Biography of Bernie Taupin

Troy R. Luther

First published by Amazon.com, Sept. 2023

Table of Contents

Introduction

In the shadowy recesses of music's past, where imagination and teamwork converge, a tale emerges that has impacted generations. It is a story told via words and music that has been expertly crafted to transcend both time and genre. This story tells of a collaboration that defied expectations and gave birth to anthems that have been ingrained in popular culture.

Bernie Taupin, whose name invokes lyrics that have started revolutions and stirred the souls of listeners, is at the center of this story. His path has been one of melody and meaning, lyric and rhythm, from the calm expanse of his youth to the electrified platforms of sold-out arenas. Beyond the tunes and the fame, however, is a person who is connected not by unrelenting ambition but rather by an insatiable hunger for artistic expression.

This isn't only a tale of cooperation; it's also an account of how one man's words left their mark on the fabric of popular culture. Bernie Taupin has been a continuous force in the ever-evolving music industry, where fads come and go with the passage of time. He represents an unfinished chapter in the history of rock 'n' roll.

As you read through these pages, you will find a story that isn't just about accomplishment but also about having the guts to express one's emotions through sound. Not only were Bernie's remarks well-chosen, but they also rang true since they were an unadulterated expression of his own experiences and perceptions. His work is seductive because it is sincere and a mirror to the complexities of life, love, and the human condition.

Bernie Taupin's narrative is a monument to the strength of commitment and vision in a society that is obsessed with rapid pleasure. It serves as an example of how tenacity and diligence can produce works of art that withstand the test of time. His experience navigating the highs and lows of the business exemplifies the incredible trajectory of a writer who persevered in the face of hardship.

You'll find stories on these pages that take you to smoke-filled studios where the magic of creation was conceived in cooperation with the mysterious Elton John. The duo's innovative dancing resulted in songs that became anthems of transformation, love, and emancipation. This isn't just a history lesson; it's an invitation to get lost in the behind-the-scenes chuckles, arguments, and collaboration that made it all possible.

This book explores the artistic expression that results when ability and inspiration come together. Building relationships has been a central theme of Bernie Taupin's career—not just with the listeners who sang his lyrics back to him but also with the songs themselves, whose lyrics became the soundtrack to countless lives.

The legacy of Bernie Taupin cannot be fully expressed in words, but you can see a little of the passion, rhythm, and feelings that inspired him to write line after line in these pages. It's a voyage that urges you to explore the depths hidden behind the lyrics, to look past the spotlights of the stage, and to enter the mind of a storyteller.

Start your journey through history, sound, and the written word now. Let Bernie Taupin's narrative serve as a reminder that brilliance does not arise from a relentless quest for fame but rather from the depth of one's soul as it is inscribed on the parchment of life. This is a story that encourages you to enter the world of songs and discover the subtleties of a life that is sung passionately and between the lines.

Remember that Troy R. Luther also wrote a spellbinding biography of Elton John as you embark on this fascinating trip through Bernie Taupin's life. The symphony of Elton's life is brought to life on the pages of "Biography of Elton John," showcasing the tunes that created his legendary career. Explore the remarkable story of Elton John's ascent to fame, his setbacks and victories, and the significant contribution he made to the music industry.

Consider losing yourself in the mellow story of Elton John's trip as you're about to discover Bernie Taupin's poetic soul. These two biographies blend together well to form a duet that invites you to witness the magic that occurs when words and music converge.

Chapter 1

Life's Starting Point

Bernie Taupin's life narrative started to take shape in the peaceful embrace of a tiny English village, molded by a familial background that would pave the way for an extraordinary trip. Bernie was raised in a modest environment, and his early years served as a blank canvas for the development of his artistic soul.

The name Bernard John Taupin CBE echoes through the halls of music history as a renowned English-American lyricist, songwriter, and visual artist. Along the way, he crosses paths with Sir Elton John, creating a songwriting partnership that will go down in the annals of success.

Taupin's life began at Flatters House, a farmhouse tucked between the villages of Anwick and Sleaford in Lincolnshire, England, where he was born on May 22, 1950. His mother Daphne and father Robert were the designers of his ancestry, and he had roots that reached far into the family tree. Daphne was descended from the eminent University of Cambridge-educated classicist John Leonard Palchett "Poppy" Cort.

The Taupin family traveled from France to London as the threads of history were being sewn, where they started a wine-importing business around the turn of the 20th century. The legacy was continued by Bernard Taupin's father, Robert Taupin, who cared for a sizable farm estate close to Market Rasen. The family relocated to a new house at Rowston Manor, a step up from the charmingly simple Flatters farmhouse that they had left behind.

Their subsequent story began in the community of Owmby-by-Spital, where they settled at Maltkiln Farm. Kit, Bernard's younger brother, was born here amidst the difficulties of rearing hens for eggs. The house was a good place to plant the seeds of creativity, even though it lacked contemporary amenities.

Bernard's career veered away from convention as he struggled with the regimented setting of school. In contrast to his brother Tony, who followed academics, Bernard's passions grew through more irrational channels. Before fate called him away, he briefly experimented in the world of print by working at The Lincolnshire Standard.

Bernard sought the excitement of youth at dances, snooker matches, and extended drives along country roads after leaving his ink-stained days behind. He found comfort in the Aston Arms bar and the allure of local life. Even still, there was a glimmer of purpose, a yearning to distinguish oneself from the crowd, among the carefree times.

At the youthful age of seventeen, Bernard noticed an advertisement at the fork in the road. This seemingly innocent choice launched him into the public eye and led him down a path where he would eventually work with none other than Elton John.

But before the spotlight and fame, Bernard's roots were in his love of books and the outdoors, a talent that had been handed down through the centuries. His early lyrical utterances were profoundly influenced by his mother's love of French literature and his grandfather's classical education. So keep in mind that Bernard John Taupin's life story is one of unanticipated turns, modest beginnings, and a commitment to follow his own special route as we travel through it.

In this tight-knit community, Bernie's early years were reminiscent of more innocent times. It was a moment of personal joy experienced at family get-togethers, shared dinners, and handwritten letters. Bernie was forever changed by these simple yet profound occurrences, which shaped his storytelling style and his exceptional capacity to capture the core of human experiences.

During those formative years, Bernie Taupin's life was a harmonious song made up of the resonant notes of his family, the natural world, and a developing artistic soul. Although his childhood was by no means lavish, it was a symphony of love, ideals, and the hope that one day his thoughts would be heard by people all across the world.

Chapter 2

Creative Alliance With Elton John

Whispers of luck's impact frequently find validity in astonishing success stories in the mysterious world of show business. This is the story of Elton John and Bernie Taupin, two legendary musicians whose names will live on in music history. With a relationship spanning more than five decades, they produced more than 50 Top 40 songs and worked their magic to sell more than 225 million records. But rather than being carefully planned, their union was created by the whims of fate.

Imagine the situation; destiny's dice are thrown onto the table. Bernie Taupin, a master wordsmith, and piano virtuoso Elton John were brought together by a mild accident rather than by any big design. Their destined pairing, which gave rise to immortal melodies and lyrical enchantment, had a beginning that was as straightforward as the luck of the draw—a tale that could only be scripted by the entertainment industry.

1967 was a pivotal year for the world's cultural change, and the atmosphere was ripe with opportunity. Two people were ready to create a relationship that would influence the soundscape for decades to come among the many people navigating the London music industry.

In quest of an elusive combination of words and melody that could turn his works into anthems, Elton John, a burgeoning artist with the natural talent to conjure melodies from piano keys, found himself. Bernie Taupin, a young lyricist who was inspired by the zeal of artistic expression, was writing rhymes across the city that rang with an honesty and depth that appeared to be almost preordained.

A period in time when the gentle currents of fate led two unique souls to a meeting that would resonate through the halls of music for decades to come. A seemingly unnoticeable advertisement appeared in the New Musical Express in the center of London's thriving music scene, where opportunity weighed heavily in the air. This modest request for talent made by Liberty Records A&R manager Ray Williams would launch a series of occasions that would eternally entangle the fates of two extraordinary people—Bernie Taupin and Elton John.

As the curtain of time rises, we see Bernie Taupin and Elton John responding to the same intriguing ad while both are pursuing their artistic goals. Their lives had been woven together in a story that was about to take place by fate, which had carefully planned this intersection.

Strangely, neither Bernie nor Elton were able to get a job with Liberty Records at first. Elton sheepishly acknowledged his inability to write lyrics when he found himself in an audition setting. In response, he was given a sealed envelope from the collection of lyrics that had been contributed; this action contained the seeds of his future. On his way home on the London Underground, Elton opened that package and found a book of poems written by none other than Bernie Taupin.

The situation was loaded with importance. It seems as though the world had planned this conversation and expertly placed Bernie's comments in Elton's hands. This seemingly unremarkable interaction served as the beginning of a collaboration that will permanently alter the musical landscape.

Over thirty albums bearing the distinct mark of their creative synergy have been the result of their flourishing relationship. But like any story of creative teamwork, their journey had its setbacks. Bernie developed his skills with other songwriters in the late 1970s, while Elton explored new musical ground with a variety of lyricists. They engaged in independent adventures after a brief break, but it was their rekindled connection that showed them the way forward.

They reunited in the music industry in the 1980s, with Bernie lending his skill with words to records like "The Fox," "21 at 33," and "Jump Up!" Bernie once again took the lead in crafting the lyrics for Elton's solo endeavors during this period, as their relationship got stronger and more progressive.

Their artistic approach, as it was described in the 1991 film "Two Rooms," had a captivating allure. In his solitary writing sessions, Bernie would let the lyrics' natural essence flourish. Then Elton would give these verses life through his music, a continuous dance that produced melodic tunes. With Bernie joining Elton in the studio for the writing and recording process, their creative relationship changed with time, strengthening the bond between their respective fields of expertise.

Their quest went beyond music, and in 2006, their musical "Lestat: The Musical" made its Broadway debut. "The Captain & The Kid," their 40th anniversary collaboration, was featured on an album cover that served as a monument to their four decades of artistic collaboration.

Their creative partnership flourished as the years passed. Audiences were enthralled by their collaborations on classic albums and movie soundtracks. Their tale was epitomized by the 2019 release of the movie "Rocketman," which showed the enduring relationship that drove their musical careers in the 1970s and 1980s.

They captured their enduring bond wonderfully in the Academy Award-winning song "(I'm Gonna) Love Me Again," penned by Bernie and

Elton. Their song served as a melodic crescendo at the closing moments of the movie "Rocketman," reflecting the profound effect of their collaboration, which defied the passage of time and crossed genre boundaries.

Their relationship developed outside of a recording studio. Their friendship flourished despite the frenzy of tours, the cheers of audiences, and the reflective moments that peppered their days. Their verbal conversation was replaced by an intuitive dance that resulted in tunes with enduring appeal.

In the case of Bernie Taupin and Elton John, their meeting wasn't just a coincidence; rather, it was the result of a celestial alignment between two creative spirits who were meant to collaborate. A famous collaboration that would forever transform the face of music was born from that first meeting; it was defined by an intangible connection that resonated through the melodies and lyrics they created together rather than just by simple collaboration.

Chapter 3

Beyond Elton John

While working with Elton John, Bernie Taupin created a musical symphony that was not limited to any one theme. Beyond the powerful chords that he and Elton created together, Bernie started his own projects and worked successfully with others, revealing other aspects of his artistic nature.

Bernie's path led him to explore his own voice by stepping into the world of solo endeavors. He dug into his own experiences and insights, using the canvas of his songs as his palette, to create storylines that bore the mark of his introspection. These solo works, free from the harmonies of a creative partner, reverberated with a sincerity that exposed the depths of his storytelling prowess.

But Bernie's interest in the arts compelled him to meet other talented people than Elton. He discovered himself working with musicians from various musical genres, adding his poetic magic to projects that covered the gamut of musical styles.

Bernie's road was studded with remarkable victories during this musical odyssey. Beyond Elton's songs, his lyrics found a home, resulting in classic songs like "We Built This City," which gained resonance through Starship's performance. With the help of English composer Martin Page, Heart's songs were given new life in "These Dreams," another lyrical masterpiece.

When Bernie co-wrote Alice Cooper's album "From the Inside" in 1978, another incredible chapter was added to the halls of musical history. This departure from his work with Elton demonstrated Bernie's talent for developing stories that went beyond his comfort zone.

Bernie's artistic abilities covered a wide range, including production. The album "American Gothic" was created in 1972 through a successful collaboration with singer-songwriter David Ackles. Despite its small sales, the record received positive reviews from critics. The significance of it was lauded by music critics; Derek Jewell of the UK Sunday Times compared it to "the Sgt. Pepper of folk." When Ackles and Elton performed together at the Troubadour in Los Angeles for Elton's American debut, the seeds of this collaboration were planted.

The written word was another medium through which Bernie's creativity was expressed. He worked with photographer Gary Bernstein to add his storytelling flair to the book "Burning Cold." His work with French American singer Josquin Des Pres resulted in the creation of an eclectic group of 13 songs in the late 1980s and early 1990s, which were accepted and sung by artists all over the world.

Bernie's band "Farm Dogs" gained a name for itself in the musical landscape in 2002 with the release of the CD "Last Stand in Open Country." Its title track was given life by Willie Nelson and Kid Rock, and it was a voyage that showed Bernie's development as an artist. Beyond the lyrics he wrote for Elton, Bernie also contributed to Willie Nelson's album "The Great Divide," which was reflected in songs like "This Face" and "Mendocino County Line."

Bernie kept looking to the future as the years painted their brushstrokes. Bernie's lyrical talent found resonance across genres, from working with Courtney Love on the moving "Uncool" to co-writing the stirring title track of Brian Wilson's Christmas album. His success reached new heights in 2006 when he shared a Golden Globe Award for the moving lyrics of "A Love That Will Never Grow Old," a song written in collaboration with Argentine producer and songwriter Gustavo Santaolalla for the movie "Brokeback Mountain."

Bernie Taupin's pursuit of songwriting went even further as he continued his creative quest. A spoken-word odyssey under the name

"Taupin" appeared in 1971, embellished with the musical tapestry spun by Davey Johnstone and Caleb Quaye, two members of Elton John's band. Listeners were guided through the lyrics of Bernie's early poems as they were delivered against a background of improvised melodies interwoven with sitar in this sonic tapestry that unfolded like a magical carpet.

"Child," the opening side of the CD, depicts Bernie's formative years in southern Lincolnshire in graphic detail. A poem called "The Greatest Discovery," which was tucked within, contained a moving viewpoint on his birth as seen by his older brother Tony. Elton John later accepted this poetic treasure and utilized it as the basis for the music on his album, "Elton John."

The album's second side revealed a mosaic of several poems, each of which had its own story to tell. Bernie's verses explored a wide range of emotions and imaginative worlds, from the musings of a puppet to the tragic narrative of a rat catcher captured by his prey. Bernie expressed his dissatisfaction in interviews despite the album's completion, showing a creative journey that had its own challenges.

Bernie's voice played a central role in the years that followed. His first studio album as a singer, "He Who Rides the Tiger," was released in the year 1980. Despite the album's melodies having resonance, it was outperformed in the charts. Later, Bernie expressed his desire for more creative control over this project, hinting at an unmet artistic need.

In 1987, with the release of the musical project "Tribe," a collaboration with Martin Page, a new chapter began. Songs like "Friend of the Flag" and "Citizen Jane" reverberated through the radio, their melodies complemented by Toni Russo's sister Rene appearing in the music videos.

A new aural environment was created in 1996 with the formation of the band "Farm Dogs," which gave Bernie's poetic sentiments life. This mellow group captured the spirit of Elton's previous work and gave it a gritty, earthy quality akin to "Tumbleweed Connection." Bernie produced fascinating storylines that evoked a distant age through his poetic tapestry, which was weaved with the music created by the band members.

The critical acclaim their debut album, "Last Stand in Open Country," received is evidence of the timeless themes Bernie's verses explored. As Willie Nelson and Kid Rock contributed their vocals to the title track's melody, giving it additional resonance, the song's resonance increased.

With the publication of "Immigrant Sons," the second and final album by Farm Dogs, in 1998, the tapestry of Bernie's solo journeys continued to unfold. Despite starting a tour around America's small stages, the album's resonance was not matched by its level of monetary success. Bernie's artistic path remained a dynamic investigation in this enthralling symphony of his solo and group ventures, a monument to his ongoing search for fresh melodies and stories that resonated far beyond the confines of his illustrious partnership with Elton John. Each new chapter of Bernie Taupin's artistic path revealed a multidimensional storyteller who weaved storylines using a variety of media. Bernie's creative inquiry went beyond the realm of music, leaving a mark on literature, photography, and even television screens, echoing the mellow cadence of his collaboration with Elton John. Bernie's mastery of poetry was evident in the book that evolved from the tapestry of 1973.

His poetry verses up to the "Goodbye Yellow Brick Road" CD were compiled in "Bernie Taupin: The One Who Writes the Words for Elton John." The book's illustrations, which were created by a variety of artists, combined Bernie's words with imaginative colors to create a visual symphony. When Bernie teamed up with rock photographer David Nutter in 1977, the beat of collaboration resounded. They collaborated to write "It's A Little Bit Funny," which perfectly encapsulated Elton John's 365-show Louder Than Concorde Tour. Through Bernie's additional narrative and Nutter's images, this now-precious book preserved the unique tapestry of Elton's adventure and is permanently in the collections of collectors.

Pages were filled to the brim with recollections of Barbados beaches, backstage get-togethers, and private moments spent with friends and renowned people. Beyond the printed word, Bernie was there. He appeared in a 1978 episode of "The Hardy Boys/Nancy Drew Mysteries," lending Shaun Cassidy his vocal backing. "A Cradle of Haloes: Sketches of a Childhood," published in 1988, was a memoir of his childhood. This personal story, which was nostalgically depicted, shed light on a magically imbued rural youth in Lincolnshire.

The story took place during the 1950s and 1960s, and it culminated with Bernie's trip to London in search of fame. Beyond the limitations of music, the lyric poet carried on with his lines. "The Devil at High Noon," a book of poetry that plays shadows and light across the pages, was self-published by Bernie in 1991. The hardcover book "Elton John & Bernie Taupin: The Complete Lyrics," a collaborative effort released in 1994, served as the culmination of his lyrics' journey.

This collection, which was colored and decorated by a variety of artists, conveyed the passage of time through echoes of the past. As he planned a fundraiser for AIDS Project Los Angeles in 1992, Bernie's creative tapestry went beyond the written word. Instead of repeating his own songs, he created a musical tableau by weaving an acoustic ensemble of classic melodies that the performers themselves had selected. Selections from "West Side Story," a musical with a timeless message of tolerance that spans decades, were played as the symphony reached its climax.

His presence echoed over the pages, images, screens, and even the hearts of those affected by his unique energy in this ongoing account of Bernie's artistic journey. Each project demonstrates his talent for using a variety of brushes and colors to paint stories, enhancing the artistic environment beyond the echoes of his cooperation with Elton.

Chapter 4

Visual Artistic Pathway

Beyond the confines of music, Bernie Taupin's imaginative symphony finds consolation and expression in the colorful brushstrokes of visual art. The year 2010 saw the start of Bernie's journey towards visual creativity, inspired by the echoes of his mother's love of the arts. His canvas grew to encompass substantial, modern assemblages, each a seamless fusion of mixed media that enticed spectators to explore their intricate tales.

Bernie's artwork has been shown in several shows and galleries from coast to coast. Its presence has reverberated with buyers and collectors alike at Art Miami, Art Southampton, and the LA Art Fair. The American flag frequently appears among the threads woven into his artistic tapestry, a symbol with multiple layers of significance.

But Bernie's journey into visual art actually began in the early 1990s, much earlier. His works made a splash in New York, Los Angeles, Chicago, and Miami, speaking to private collectors who connected with his visual story. His most recent solo show, "8," covered the walls of KM Fine Arts in Los Angeles and mesmerized viewers with its splendor and masterworks of mixed media.

Bernie's artwork gave the backdrop of an election fresh vitality amidst the shifting tides of the seasons. The American flag was depicted in galleries, serving as a visual reminder of the numerous details that make up the fabric of the country. This voyage wasn't just a passing experience for Bernie; it was a constant desire that powered him from the inside out.

Both of these artistic endeavors, for Bernie, were parallel to the beat of his music and were means of self-expression. He used found objects and assemblage elements in his work with the intention of guiding viewers on an exploratory trip. He rejected the derogatory moniker of "celebrity artist," believing that the value of his work was demonstrated by the acclaim it received.

Bernie's artistic development followed the course of the 1960s and 1970s American modernist movements. He discovered that his medium was changing, adopting a tactile orientation, from painting to sculpting. He used a variety of media as his canvas, giving his works of art life with objects like eight-track recordings, guitar picks, old comic books, and Polaroids. His story benefited from a touch of edge and sharp societal commentary.

Bernie's creative method involved a balancing act between ideas and actions. The canvas on which he painted was the initial spark of an idea, and once lit, the execution came easily. His mind continued to be a continual creator even during dry periods, awakening him in the middle of the night with visions that begged to be fulfilled.

Bernie assumed the role of a contemporary alchemist in his studio, which was filled with mediums and music. He put his soul into each creation as he brought his thoughts to reality, and the hours flew by. His studio served as his haven, a place where he could express himself freely through innovation and creation.

The story of Bernie's path into visual art resounded with the spirit of a crazy professor, a creator propelled by a burning desire to express themselves. With each brushstroke, he painted stories that spoke to the core of who he was—a painter who had discovered his canvas outside of musical melodies.

Chapter 5

Personal Life

Bernie Taupin's personal life moved to its own beat away from the spotlight and the songs, exposing a canvas painted with relationships, difficulties, and the myriad threads of existence. His own life developed in its own distinct chapters, much like the stories that his poems reflected.

The story of Bernie Taupin's journey through love and marriage played out like a series of chapters, each with its own emotional melody. He entered the dance of matrimony four times, each coupling creating its own unique symphony.

Maxine Feibelman's arrival in 1971 marked the start of his heart's voyage; their harmonies continued for five years before vanishing. As the pages of love turned further, Toni Lynn Russo entered his life in 1979. Through the early 1990s, their rhythm continued to reverberate for more than ten years. Then came Stephanie Haymes Roven, whose love story spanned the years 1993 to 1998 and was woven into the fabric of her own family. But once more, the colorful tapestry of love came into view, introducing Bernie to Heather Kidd in March 2004. In California's coastal winds, where they built a life together and had two daughters, Charley Indiana and Georgey Devon, their bond developed.

Bernie's transoceanic journey was an adventure that vividly colored his identity. The United

States, a country that called with its own songs and prospects, was where he set sail. In 1990, he had a shift as he accepted his new citizenship and home, finding meaning in the tones of the American environment.

Bernie's contented life was set against a Santa Barbara County, California, backdrop. He discovered a haven where his creative soul flourished, fusing the echoes of his music and his art with the gorgeous surroundings and soothing seas.

The peak of Bernie's voyage came in 2022, when his musical contributions reverberated across the halls of fame. It was a monument to the songs he had woven into the world's fabric that he was named Commander of the Order of the British Empire (CBE) in the New Year's Honours.

The numerous songs that shaped Bernie Taupin's identity were evident as his life story wove through marriages, citizenship, and honors. The journey had its ups and downs, but it was still a sincere piece that reflected the rhythm of life.

Chapter 6

Awards and Recognitions

The legacy of Bernie Taupin is a tapestry made of his poetic brilliance, artistic discovery, and steadfast relationships. His influence on the worlds of music and art is more than just a passing nod; it is a ringing tune that will last throughout time.

His successful collaboration with Elton John, which gave rise to some of the most well-known songs in music history, is at the core of his career. From "Your Song" to "Rocket Man," their joint efforts left stories of love, yearning, and life imprinted on the collective memory of generations. Their songs resonated through time, space, and cultures, leaving an enduring imprint on the tapestry of popular music.

Bernie's aesthetic efforts expanded his legacy in addition to his poetic contributions. His artistic works, which combined several genres and plots, vividly depicted feelings and stories. Each work of his art is a dialogue between the canvas and the viewer that invites them to explore the work's depths.

Elton John and Bernie Taupin paved a way that has endured throughout time. In 1992, their mellow journey brought them to the prestigious Songwriters Hall of Fame. Their tunes' chords were entangled with the history of time, leaving their names in folklore.

The pinnacle of Bernie's artistic prowess materialized in 2020, a year that reverberated with acclaim. They collaborated to create "(I'm Gonna) Love Me Again," which was honored with the prestigious Oscar for Best Original Song. Their musical alchemy had attained a pinnacle that touched people's hearts and souls and solidified their legacy.

As the years passed, Bernie's journey kept developing. As his legacy reverberated through the Rock & Roll Hall of Fame, the year 2023 marked the beginning of a new chapter in his story. He was given the Musical Excellence Award, a recognition of the tunes' power to transform the lives of countless listeners.

Beyond the confines of honors and acclaim, Bernie left a lasting legacy. It endures in the hearts of people who have connected with him through his music, found peace in his lyrics, and found inspiration in his artwork. His melodies are companions to both joy and sadness; they are more than just songs; they are anthems of life's events.

As the years pass, Bernie's legacy endures as a constant song that is still sung, cherished, and welcomed. His influence on the artistic world cannot be assessed solely in terms of notes or strokes but also in terms of the feelings, narratives, and resonance he has sparked in the hearts of millions.

Conclusion

The symphony of Bernie Taupin's life continues until the last note fades into silence, leaving behind a legacy that resonates across the annals of musical history and beyond. A tapestry of artistic creativity that transcends boundaries and captures the essence of human feeling has been woven by his journey, which has been characterized by poetry lyrics and visual manifestations.

In addition to writing lyrics, Bernie is remembered alongside the greats for creating stories that millions of people could identify with. His collaboration with Elton John is a unique chapter in songwriting collaboration that transcends time and genre boundaries. From the moving "Your Song" to the song "Don't Let the Sun Go Down on Me," their works have crossed generations, connecting with people on a familiar level.

However, Bernie's influence goes well beyond the lyrics that embellished Elton John's musical compositions. Another aspect of his creative legacy is his visual work, which is a dance of colors and feelings. He created stories that spoke to the viewer's soul with each stroke, inviting them to explore the complexities of reality through the lens of his imagination. His talent for the arts is evidence of how rich his creative wellspring is.

Each distinction served as a note of confirmation in the symphony of Bernie's career, adorning his journey of recognition. His services to music are crowned by the honorific title of Commander of the Order of the British Empire (CBE), which reverberates throughout history. The Rock and Roll Hall of Fame's Musical Excellence Award honors the depths of his artistic genius, and his admission into the Songwriters Hall of Fame is a monument to the tunes that molded people's hearts and minds.

But Bernie's influence extends beyond the music industry. His life is an investigation into interpersonal dynamics and the cyclical nature of existence. Marriages and divorces, difficulties and victories—these are all strands of his life story that give his legacy more complexity. His capacity for navigating life's challenges and still producing art that has meaning demonstrates the complexity of his spirit.

The core of Bernie's legacy is found in his capacity for relating. His songs serve as conduits that connect feelings, moments, and experiences across time and location rather than just being simple compositions. His songs have accompanied people on the path of life through joy, sadness, love, and pain, understanding when words falter, and providing comfort when hearts ache.

The tune lingers as this story's final chapter is being penned. The legacy of Bernie Taupin is woven into the very fabric of artistic expression, transcending the boundaries of a book's pages. His songs will still be played on radios, in concert halls, and around campfires. His works of art will continue to arouse thought and reflection and to start conversations off the canvas.

The permanent resonance of Bernie more than his momentary stardom is what makes an impression. It's about the connections he cultivated, the relationships he forged, and the stories he told. His legacy is an anthem to creation that never fails to uplift, an homage to the ability of art to break down borders and bring people together via a common experience.

As we put a bow on Bernie Taupin's journey, let us keep in mind that his melodies will always be heard in our hearts, his lyrics will always ring in our heads, and his artwork will always evoke strong emotions in us. His legacy endures, bearing witness to the enduring value of artistic expression and the unyielding character of a man who gave voice to the beauty and complexity of the human experience.

Remember to purchase "The Biography of Elton John" by Troy R. Luther to know about Elton John's life.

Printed in Great Britain
by Amazon

30626420R00031